My Diary and other Poems

Ishika Bansal

DIAMOND BOOKS
www.diamondbook.in

Publisher	:	Diamond Pocket Books (P) Ltd. X-30, Okhla Industrial Area, Phase-II New Delhi-110020
Phone	:	011-40712200
E-mail	:	wecare@diamondbooks.in
Website	:	www.diamondbooks.in
Edition	:	2026

My Diary and other Poems

Author: Ishika Bansal

Dedication

This book is gratefully dedicated to senior Poet Mr. Rajiv Khandelwal who has always helped and guided me in my poetic journey and always motivates me to better myself and grow higher and higher.

Foreword-1

"My Diary and other Poems"- is yet another vibrant kaleidoscope of youthful impressions and expressions! I can't but be glad to see Ishika's pen sprout out poetry again. Her wit and verbal jugglery is undoubtedly impressive in this collection. The poems have a wide range from personal reflection to confessions to awareness of her surroundings and insightful axioms. It has been a delight to peruse this 'fun-filled' anthology.

My congratulations, for this second brainchild of hers.

Yet, dear Ishika, I need to mention that success has kissed your feet while they are yet tender. You are very fortunate to be blessed with a flair and have an opportunity to emblazon it in print. I am glad that your pen has become so free and frequent, spurting poetry as a fresh water spring.

Nevertheless my dear, there is no such thing as a free lunch and hence success too has a price. It ensnares young poetic sensibilities with the glitz of popularity and leadership. Make sure that you never start writing for the public but for your own heart. Your poetry does show some candid present reflection, but honestly, many times while reading, I felt that the verse is cast in the same mould as the previous collection, *"Threads of Life"*.

So my advice: Don't be in a hurry to get printed. As you grow, poetry will ripen within you without effort. Remember, poetry is alive, it breathes, it grows, it matures on its own. I hope I am not being too critical or discouraging, but I can see some unearthed potential still in you. Give it time to bloom.

P. S. :- Some pieces from *"My Diary and other Poems"* are real gems. Go ahead and get the collection printed. For the next one, pay careful attention to syntax and try to write from someone else's standpoint, be someone else's voice or create a socially conscious poetic persona.

And finally my best wishes from the treacherous waters of popularity.

Ms Nevidita Lal

English Language Teacher

St. Conrad's Inter College, Agra

Foreword-2

Child is father of man- may have been an enigma in the literary spheres but it is a proven fact that a student of eighth class writes so well sometimes to peck the tall trees of Kabir's thought regarding 'words' as especially chosen to be translated by the noble laureate Rabindranath Tagore. Ishika Bansal has devoted two of her poems at the beginning to 'words' and their significance and magnificence. Almost all connotations of the 'words' have been summarized in brevity except the Kabir's spiritual and philosophic optimization. The metaphor of 'flowing river which never comes into hold' is beautiful as compared to the 'stream of consciousness' often used in the literature.

'My Diary' is representative of contemporary surroundings of a student and 'My Hustling Class' and 'Childhood' speak about the innocence' which is still housed by the adolescence and infancy. Although the poem 'Speak Out' is short but the idea conceived is magnanimous and contains universe within it. The dedication of the poem goes to the goddess of speech- may be Gayatri or Sarasvati in the later years but the birth of civilizations owes its debt to the human speech- may be innovative or absurd. Let us have a look at the opening two lines:

"Don't let any idea remain unheard
May be innovative or absurd..."

Innocence and introspection streaks the poetic thought of Ishika Bansal, the poem may be 'That's How I Am' or 'Find out 'Me' Time' sordid surroundings do haunt the innocent mind to react in poems like 'A Sneak Look Outside' and 'The other Side of Today's World' and the reaction is certainly not childish rather it is perceived and conceived analysis of the contemporary world. She has depicted a mad race, the individualistic attitude, the boasting of the opulence, and all the malice of the fake world of today which is eulogized as 'modern world liberalization and globalization' but obviously based on survival of the fittest without any emotional quotient.

Ishika Bansal maintains the literary standards of an evolved poet in alliteration when she writes – 'To evolve envy and enmity' besides the rhythm and rhyme in her poem 'Be An Actor Not a Reactor.' The idea developed by the young poet is lofty and she has lived upto the demands of the readers who find novelty and freshness in staging a contrast of paradoxical anecdotes. Sometimes the poems touch didactic note as in the poem 'Hardships' Ishika turns to preach solutions in the face of odds, but the impressionistic mind has imbibed good qualities from her teachers and parents which have been churned within to be expressed aloud in her poetic narration. In the same breath is written 'Impressions' and 'Embellish up Your Future.' To have taste of her learning and expression, enjoy the stanza:

> "The past is gone, the present is going
> And the future is still in our hands,
> Stand up for winning one day
> The odds of life will forever end."

Ishika Bansal has laid emphasis on the 'originality' and wants to compete with the stars to shine like a 'shimmering sun' and she has successfully made an attempt to be abreast of her times, particularly of her age, education and experience. She has miles to go in her journey of life and the poems penned by her like 'Trust Your Instincts' speak volumes about her zeal to cross the hurdle race of life with brilliance and she would be star poet in few years to come as almost all the topics chosen by her for writing poems are of high denomination and calibre. She has spurned mundane thought, introspected herself, looked within, contemplated to conceive noble ideas, added freshness to the literature and its foliage. The diction is good with its natural flow but editing is conspicuous with its absence as full stop and comas are missing.

I wish and welcome the young budding poet Ishika Bansal to bloom in the fragrant garden of poetic thought and provide bunch of muse to the readers.

Mr. Anil Sharma
Editor: Contemporary Vibes
On My Diary and other Poems

Praise for Ishika Bansal

Ishika is a precocious child writing matured poetry. Her exquisitely crafted poetry is eminently readable.

Apparently she is a poet with rare vision and extraordinary talent. All her poetry is deep in thought and clever in expression. She is a keen observer of life, nature and people, and is quite efficient in rearranging the same in a beautiful verse form that stands the toughest test of her times. She writes brilliantly about her subtle thoughts, her strong reactions, and very many things that she finds in her neighborhood together with her feelings about her Mom and Dad.

To get the full view of her poetic profile, one has to read her poetry. Nevertheless she is a complete poet. I wish she continues writing.

In her poetry we find beautiful images and astonishing narrative. She avoids repetition which is good for her and her poetry. Repetition is a retarding process and a sign of regression, she perhaps knows this fact.

Her determination to get over the difficulties in life, her positiveness, her wish to write better and excel in poetry, her human concern, her optimism, perseverance, consistency in thought and constancy in her attempts will certainly go a long way to help her achieve what she is striving for.

Her poetry as we come across in this book, is spontaneous, hilarious, imaginative, miraculous, and a natural overflow of her passionate feelings rather than mere impulsiveness. And as she reveals in one of her poems, she is her own guide. There is no external binding as such.

Check out some of the key lines that are self explanatory - The world is going to wait; I, me, myself, my own poetic image; I dream and desire to conquer the world, and 'I agree to be 'me'. These are the utterances of a bright, intelligent, sensitive , inventive, wide-awake, and whiz kid Ishika Bansal who transcends her childhood to reach the moon, that is, her poetic heights, without caring for the usual impediments.

Ishika's poetry is so elegant, so natural, and so wise, and so promising!

Dr Kailash Chander
Poet, Critic and Advisor to Poetry Journals

Keeping in view the age and experience of Ishika Bansal, one can easily say that she is a budding poet. She seems to have begun her literary career promisingly with short meaningful poems that touch almost all vital aspects of life. Capturing even minor experiences of life and presenting them with unprecedented aesthetic beauty is a rare phenomenon not easily conceivable in any child of her age. For a little girl to be gifted with keen observation, deep insight, rare aesthetic vision and profound wisdom, show how God has bestowed His choicest blessings on her. Like great optimists, she is also optimistic about life and its future:

A new light to shine once again
A new vision to grief and pain
A new hope to the ignorant
A new start for the brain.

I'm sure, a day will soon come when she will take our literary world by storm. I soulfully wish her all success in life.

Dalip Khetarpal,
Author, poet, critic, reviewer,
short story writer and columnist. Ambala.

Comments

Such meaningful lines at her young age reflect Ishika's originality of thoughts and a pure heart. Her poems emote the broad spectrum of human sensibilities and have an aura of innocence & sensitivity of a budding poetess.

Sadhana Bhargava
Poetess & Short Story Writer, Agra

With multilateral charisma Ishika Bansal is a philoprogenitive poetess. She has a sublime control on language. Her poems heave from the contemplation of life. She writes with a pictorial finality, illustrating with her phrases varied kind of sensations.

Her erudition of soul resounds in her poetry. Her writings endue versus unfolding novice facets of conscience. Her poems are epos of vitality, reflectivity and pathos. Her creative brilliance distinctly exhibits in her poetry.

I hope that this queer compilation of her verses install a affinity with the readers and imprint incorrigible mark on their psyche.

Pummy Sadana
Poetess, Agra

I am impressed with your range Ishika, Good Job. All the poems are beautiful, full of thought & relate-able. Keep it up child. U'll bloom as a prolific poetess. Lots of Love and blessings

Roli Sinha
Poetess, Agra

Sense and Sound in Ishika's Poetic Effusions

Ishika Bansal's second anthology of verses reveals a mature poet in her. She has developed not only a better art of painting words but also the focusing of sense and sound in her outpourings.

Hers is the poetic world in which she delves deep into her imaginations, emotions and expresses a wide-range of experiences and observations of life. A good amount of similes and metaphors add a great degree of poetic sensibility to her poetic effusions. Her attitude to life and to the people around is very pragmatic:

> Copying moves along with people in crowd,
> Keep up the originality with which you're endowed.

*****

> What difference you add to your efforts
> Is what you receive.

She, like a mentor, is able to give the message of being the one among many:

> Beautiful made by many, masterpieces by one.

*****

The poet comes forward as a friend, philosopher and guide, and proves that, being a budding poet, she is equally mature and capable of conveying what Rudyard Kipling has opined in his poetic piece “If”.

She says:

> Remember the fools will open up
> To evolve envy and enmity.

*****

> Don’t care what people say …

The psycho-maturity of Ishika is, indeed, praise worthy and worth quoting:

> But you have to turn this game;
> Wickedly into your favour
> By smiling and understanding them as a joke.

Her metaphorical expressions are marvellous. In the poem ‘Childhood’ the poet paints:

> If these freshly planted seeds
> Watered with guidance and appreciation
> Can become what they dream.

*****

Ishika’s poems are replete with the sense of wit and wisdom, love of mature, deep concern for goodness in people, significance of time, self-elevation, psychotherapy, the role of family and father, quest for self, paramount place of music in life, etc. that makes her a multi-dimensional figure amongst the so called crowd of emerging budding creative artists in literature.

Her sacramental upbringing is clearly visible in her expression for her teachers. She is honest in expressing her own self:

> Very lively, friendly, a little self obsessed me.

*****

So that freaky, strange I am.

The latent seeds of ambition in the poet for upcoming future makes her such an aspirant as will certainly reach her destination. This is her positivity of personality. She opines:

A future icon, an activist, the world reformer.

*****

To sum up, I would like to say that the poet is well aware and conscious of mortality of the world, utmost need of pollution free-environment, social bonds of love and faith, significance of human behaviour and dealings between man and man and women empowerment etc.

I sincerely suggest her not to avoid punctuation to the extent that her expression lose the worth they possess.

I wish Ishika a very bright future as a poet and litterateur.

October 16,2018

Dr. R.S. Tewari 'Shikhresh'
Assistant Director (O.L.) Income Tax Dept. Agra
A Poet and Critic

Some Observations

It is stated that: "Words can inspire. And words can destroy. Choose yours well." It is also said that:- "You can change the course of your life with your words" and Ishika at such a young age not only understand this but also believes:

> … They can bring in a lot of change
> Depends on how we use them
> Work with them wisely
> They are words

Words 1

H. Scott Momaday said that: "If you believe in the power of words, you can bring about physical changes in the universe." Ishika also thinks on similar lines:

> They are the source
> By which we can resolve a query
> And a friendship start
> It is the way which can both hurt anybody
> Or win the feelings of one's heart
> By expressing the feelings of our heart with someone
> We can reduce our stress …

Words 2

Keeping a diary means writing down what happened and this writing can be used to relieve stress as it allows one to reflect, to explore our true selves, understand ourselves and become our best versions through growing personally, and Ishika understands this:

... All my secrets, lies and truths
Are suffused in you ...

... When I open, write and close you
I feel a lot of satisfaction

My Diary

Environment plays a critical role in the development of children, and Ishika is conscious about it and observes that in Childhood:

... If these freshly planted seeds
Are watered with guidance and appreciation
Can become what they dream ...

Childhood

Psychologists are now a-days advocating that in this materialistic world the demands on one's time can be overwhelming in their routinized jam-packed schedules and thus securing some time for oneself is a must. Stress and the inability to enjoy a little time-out, can have a real negative health and psychological effects. A little "me" time can make one a better person both inside and out.

And Ishika at this young age realizes this and pens her poem Find Out 'Me' Time.

In her Poem "Loneliness – A Great Phase In Life", she voices:

...Sometime I like and enjoy myself sitting alone...
... That's why I like staying alone
To supervise myself, to help
Me-myself and staying away from pointless tension

Loneliness – A Great Phase In Life

She actually uses "Me Time" when she says in her poem, "Zero Period":

> ...Pin-drop silence, not a word do I utter
> This time is for me
> To know myself better
>
> Zero Period

Ishika comes across as a very optimistic girl when in her poem, Each Day, New Light says:

> ... A new chance to dream big
> A new day to excel ...

Or in her poem "Be An Actor Not A Reactor" when she says:

> ... At last you'll surely win
> If you never lose hope
> If you scour something positive
> In every negative phase of life
> And if learnt from darkness to cope
>
> Be An Actor Not A Reactor

At her age, when most of her contemporary students are grappling with imagination, words, phrases, devices, talent, Ishika seems to display a certain mature level of Imagination and reliance in her word-weaving and displays a rather good awareness of poetic devices. She uses concrete imagery in her poem "Where Am I?"

> ... In the folded, personalized pages, I am...
> .. In the blue sky
> In the green meadow, I am..

In her poem, “Trust your Instincts”, she uses the poetic device of alliteration: “And shine like the shimmering sun”. We also see an example of alliteration in her poem “My Worthy Hand”: “Smelly, sweaty, sticky”.

In my opinion, she is competent to stir a reader’s imagination and his/her emotions and can construct realistic world for her readers. Some of her poems have powerful messages expressed in impressive ways. Since this is not intended as an extended, in-depth review article, I will sum up using the above examples that Ishika shows a maturity beyond her age – shows an honesty of emotions in her thought content, has a good vocabulary, has a way with words that gets displayed via an active Imagination, and she is slowly but surely learning to use the resources of poetic language to capture various situations in a manner that shows she is not challenged at all at an age, when most of her contemporary students would be challenged in penning a simple poem.

I hope she can find the time from her academic commitments to read more and more poetry and books on the Art & Craft of poetry writing, and uses more and more poetic tools in her future creative writings.

Rajiv Khandelwal
Senior Poet, Agra

Author's Note

It's nothing less than a dream for me to get up one day and see all my write-ups compiled in a book for the first time and yet again with the second one is surreal. The whole process of writing your thoughts out on paper is as real as spurting yourself and putting yourself out there. All my poems, my articles, my write-ups are as dear to me as an infant is to its mommy. I literally adore them, they're like the little awards that I have accumulated over the years. Poetry for me is very special and the art of nurturing it just makes my presence felt. Most importantly, I can be who I am, in the process of it engulfing me and engrossing me in a way to bring out the best in me. Either to pen my words on paper, to string them in a meter or to spunk them with metaphors and similes, it is so engaging in itself that it betters me with every session I have with it.

This book "My Diary And Other Poems" carries a sharp reflexion of my personality and day-to-day life and it is magnificently turned out. Honestly, poetry, specially in the past one year made me grow to an unreal extent. I now can bravely face situations; can be truly happy from within and can be confident about myself and life. Poetry taught me many things and has given me a lot for which I am eternally grateful to it.

At last I would like to thank my family. My mum who always keeps me grounded, my dad without whose continuous inspiration and admiration my world would have shattered. My grandparents who always teach me to share love and care for others and at last my brother whose unlikable and sarcastic comments made me more likable.

Rajiv Khandelwal Uncle, I couldn't thank him enough for his continuous efforts for my book and his humble spirit for shaping the poetic world around me.

My special thanks to Prof Bhupinder Parihar ji for his support and editorial corrections.

And thanks to all the editors who published my poems in their journals.

With this book I learn more about love, laughter and gratification.

Hoping for many others.

-Ishika Bansal

Email: ishikab233@gmail.com

Insta: poeticeffusions

Blog : www.mypoetiicendeavours.wordpress.com

Preface

As the reader holds this anthology of verse in his/her hands, the curiosity will naturally tickle her/him to ask a question: What is the purpose behind this book of poems by a high school girl? The simple answer is: It is to make the reader enter the introspective phase of cerebral ferment in the teen years. The young poet Ishika Bansal has chosen to direct her creative energies and intellect to nurture values which stimulate idealism, and a passion for critical education. It is the range of aptitude and potential we as humans realize with a purpose. Poetry is a form of contemplation, the highest human ability and distinction.

The poems in this anthology imply a human centered world-view in which actions and activities are of supreme value. The world around us may be is a place of conflict – a place where 'ignorant armies clash by night', but the human worth is measured against individual endeavour. The individual effort essentially forms the bedrock of lives we live. It is in schools we create and promote a child-centric world, where latent potential can be sparked and nurtured, and wedded into the fabric of our thought and action. This is something so vital that we cannot leave it to chance.

As is obvious in these poems, the scope of poetry is much more wider. Varied ideas, feelings, messages are woven into a few lines. The poems prod us to imagine that we all are poets – budding poets blessed with delicate seeds of creativity, though in the germ. The poems communicate; they force us to reflect and change. They serve a purpose; shape and redefine our thoughts, and highlight the significance of poetry:

Don't let any idea remain unheard
May be innovative or absurd
Our speech decides the strength we possess
So, speak out, be aloud
May be you convince someone one day

'Speak Out'

...They can bring in a lot of change
Depends on how we use them
Work with them wisely
They are words

'Words-1'

...At least you'll surely win
If you never lose hope
If you scour something positive
In every negative phase of life
And if learn from darkness to cope

'Be an Actor Not Reactor'

Edward de Bono, a leading creative thinker when asked: "Why we need creativity," replied: "Because computers will do everything else." Our thoughts are fleeting, but words in poetry become tangible; they acquire power, call an abstract idea, nurture original thinking, widen our perceptions, light the most mundane. The power of imagination is incredible. The poems in this collection cajole the reader to give poetry a chance. There is variety; they make the reader pause to reflect. One of the functions of poetry is to help us make sense of ourselves in the world. Therefore, poetry writing and poetry reading should be an integral part of the education of the young people who, particularly in the adolescent years have difficulty in making sense of themselves as their inner world is centripetal.

In 2005, the Division of Higher Education, UNESCO published a document on Teachers Education titled "Reading and Writing Poetry". Ishika is a practicing poet, and practice has no end. The point she stresses is why poetry needs to be a part of our growing years. Her poetry is a reflection of the world and humankind, and that imagination is a creative discipline that can be cultivated over the years with sensitive perception, observation, commentaries and above all with the stark encounters with life. Ishika Bansal interprets and decodes the dilemmas of life – at such a young age – is something amazing.

The young poet is beyond rote learning. For her, education is a liberal art, an imaginative exercise beyond the calculations of day-to-day living. In a way, she has encouraged the education system to get into learning the primary systems of educational ethos. The poet's effort is to cultivate an environment that can contribute to the world. In the process, the poet attempts to understand her own self. Her exposure to poetry writing is an exposure to a culture that is universally shared.

Ishika Bansal as poet has played a game with language which training over the years will polish and chasten. She has used words – this is something extraordinary. Her poetry is a reflection of her sensitivity to the freedom to explore the world around her, and her own self. Praise and criticism go together which make the poem vibrant and accessible:

> …Let's wake people in deep slumber
> Within our range
> Looking out
> Let's urge for a change
>
> 'A Sneak Look Outside'

...Let us be high now, let others get demotion
This race is making people insane
And making them forget emotion

'The Other Side of Today's World'

Poetry is an individual response that encourages the reader to think. My Diary poem is a spontaneous poem, loaded with meaning. The collection is an invitation to connect, to invite school going adolescents on a regular basis for poetry sessions and established poetry clubs and publishing poetry magazines. The members will have the feel that they have entrusted themselves to a creativity.

Ishika Bansal's poems have another effect – the desire to change – inner and outer. They inspire the reader to be better human beings. She addresses problems sincerely and objectively and encourages to seek solutions for themselves. Grounded in both sensibility and intellect, the poems appeal through emotions – an emotional equivalent of thought. The combination of words and ideas embodies an understanding of the essence of human culture:

...Tremendous efforts, vision in eyes
This is all I need in life to rise

'Impressions'

The best way to predict the future
Is to create it ...

'Embellish Up Your Future'

...We should, we must, we can
Let our words do all the magic
As our clothes don't make the man

'Clothes Don't Make a Man'

Philip Sidney (in 1580) logically defends poetry, and proves that poetry deserves the "laurel crown". Sydney's plea is that poetry should be restored to its honourable place because of its antiquity, its universality, and the high esteem it has enjoyed from antiquity. Ben Jonson (1573-1637) highlights the instructional functions of poetry in these words:

"It nourishes and instructs our youth; delights our age, adorns our prosperity, comforts our diversity, entertains us at home, keeps us company abroad, travels with us..."

John Dryden (1631-1700) is his essay on Dramatic poesy (1668) remarked:

"Poetry is a just and lively image of human nature, representing the passions and humours, and the change of fortune to which it is subject, for the delight and instructions of mankind…"

This obviously means poetry is not just a tasteful arrangement of words, images and rhythm and rhymes and other characteristics of language. What is poetry writing for? Expression. Poetry language has a primary function (in human affairs) of conveying meaning:

…A new chance to dream big
A new way to excel

'Each Day, New Light'

A day productive feels like
Cherry on the cake….

'A Day That Went Productive'

For Shelley, imagination is the indispensable agency of all poetic creation. Shelley remarked:

"A poem is the very image of life expressed in its external truth… it is the creation of actions according to the unchangeable forms of human nature, as existing in the mind of the creator, which is itself the image of all other minds".

During the Victorian age, Matthew Arnold (1822-1888) asserted the value of poetry as antidote to the cultural anarchy of the age. For Arnold, poetry is at the bottom "Criticism of Life". Today, in our globalised postmodern world, poetry has the power and potential of facing the onslaught of commerce and consumerism, industry and technology. Poetry adds charm to the business of life. Ishika Bansal as poet is interested in recording the happy play of impulses on particular occasions:

> ...Just push pillows aside
> And come out of your beds
> The chirping, whispering birds
> Are waiting for you...
>
> 'Dawn Time'

> ...The cosy breeze striking against my face
> The adorable birds racing in pace ...
> Oh, I'll rush home the sun is about to set
>
> 'A Day On The Beach'

I .A. Richards in the twentieth century defined a poem as a collection of experiences of a poet. But, no single experience makes a poem; a poem is an amalgam of experiences. Experiences occasioned by words create a world-view – a moral theory of art. Richards took rigorous interest in the verbal analysis of poetry as poetic structures hold the key to meaning and message, the point of view, i.e., the authorial projection.

The school-going students can learn a lot from this collection "My Diary and Other Poems". The poems urge and encourage the idea of keeping journals and diaries in which they enter their thoughts and images. They make a note of anything out of ordinary that occurs to them, including phrases, expressions, experiences etc. An interest in the nuts and bolts of language is vital to anyone in understanding and composing poetry.

It is also vital that a student is exposed to contemporary poets in the classroom. Poets, particularly those who can connect with adolescents may be invited into schools wherever feasible. This will generate a climate. One major effect of poetry is to change how we look at the world; it metamorphoses readers and listeners into sensitized beings.

These poems deals with topics within the area of interest of the target group of young people, the efforts must go on:

> …Our dynamic struggle blossoms at last
> Sometimes so stubborn
> Sometimes so fast …
>
> 'A Fresh Poem'

> …We are all moody and truly insane
> The innocence lies in this hustle and bustle
> Which will not be renewed again
>
> 'My Hustling Class'

> …I am with my quirky friends
> In their giggles and pranks, I am
> I am in the mesmerizing content of a book
> In the tossed, marinated, fresh poem, I am
>
> 'Where Am I'

> …This hunt has given me
> A lot of growth and new dreams
> I am in search of more
> I'll be one as a team
>
> 'In Search of More'

...So, let ourselves do something
While the world waits

'The World Is Going To Wait'

Poetry magnifies life; offers space and the freedom to choose a language for both self-expression and enjoyment. Human behavior is changing. The need is to understand ourselves and our environment; this will help personal development and the willingness to contribute to the world around.

I hope the young readers will connect with these situations. The famous French poet Paul Valéry remarked: "Poetry cannot be taught, it can only be studied". Poetry has to be felt for what it is. That is the reason poetry has deep connections with music and art.

The beauty of the poems in "My Diary and Other Poems" is that the poet takes us along on a fantastic journey at such a young age. She lights the most mundane, builds a microcosm, impels the imagination to recreate the familiar and the known – all this within seconds. The collection though in no way reflects erudite scholarship or the knowledge of metrics. The poems are simple and effortless; there is variety, but there is seriousness too.

I do hope the readers enjoy leafing through the pages of the collection "My Diary and Other Poems". Here is wishing the poet an enlightened life, and opportunities to write more poems. Amen!

Bhupinder Aziz Parihar
Shiromani Litterateur
Former Professor & Head
Post Graduate Department of English
Government College, Ludhina, Punjab.

Contents

Words 1

They are spontaneous
Hilarious, miraculous
Can be harsh and discourteous
Are inspiring, surprising
Life-changing, sporadically depressing
Sometimes shattering, at times daring

They can bring in a lot of change
Depends on how we use them

Work with them wisely
They are words.

Words 2

They are the source
By which we can resolve a query
And a friendship start
It is the way which can both hurt anybody
Or win the feelings of one's heart
By expressing the feelings of our heart with someone
We can reduce our stress
We can shape a good personality
By judging how polite we are
And how good words we possess
Words used in a good manner are like gold
But they are like a flowing river
Which never comes into hold.

My Diary

I possess you, a simple, surly diary
Yet I can adorn you
With all my joy and stress

You're thick and heavy
But better than teddies and toys
I can share if someone makes my day
Or if someone annoys

All my secrets, lies and truths
Are suffused in you
But when someone opens you up
You are always kind and true

When I open, write and close you
I feel a lot of satisfaction
And all your drafted sheets
Track my every position and action.

My Hustling Class

A lot of noise, teachers yelling at us
Most probably the fish market
Or the travellers coming out of the bus

Whistling, whispering and gossiping all around
Some are extremely happy
For no reason some are frowned

All good dancers, phenomenal singers
And great orators are here
Some are shining stars
Some are stepping gears

We are all moody and truly insane
The innocence lies in this hustle and bustle
Which will not be renewed again.

Childhood

Childhood is filled with innocence and naïve looks
Children are strands of imagination
Are to be embellished
By keeping them away
From all hooks and crooks

The fragrance of love and care
Scattered all around
A little mischievous is their behaviour
A little sweet they sound
If these freshly planted seeds
Are watered with guidance and appreciation
Can become what they dream
But if this childhood is gone in vain
Nobody for sure is going to redeem it

From these memories, sometimes thrill
Sometimes joy I attain
But, the devastating point is
They cannot be relived again.

Speak Out

Don't let any idea remain unheard
Maybe innovative or absurd
Our speech decides the strength we possess
So, speak out, be aloud
Maybe you convince someone one day.

A Creation

My personification of the piece of literature I write
Close to my heart, the world of thoughts I imbibe
Thudding of my heart in sequence which runs
My soul feels alive, a new creation being done

The charm on my face, earlier I persuade
From the sun scorching to soothing shade
Seems like from the whole world I've won
My soul feels alive, a new creation being done.

That’s How I Am

I, me, myself, my own poetic guide
Sometimes I grapple with words
Sometimes with tunes I abide

Love reading books
But sometimes for my exams, I cram
Don’t take me amiss
But that’s how I am

Very lively, friendly, a little self-obsessed me
Always positivity around, I try to see
Sometimes nervous and embarrassed I am
So, that freaky, strange I am

A little mature in my poems
More than childish at home
What’s more often clueless I am
No matter what, that’s how I am.

Find Out 'Me' Time

Don't abandon your mundane pleasure in haste
Don't let any complexity compel
You to leave your zest

Don't let anything bother you
Don't engross in hustle that much
That you quit all peace and rest
Don't leave distressing behind
When busy reaching the crest

Don't forget to trace things that please you
Don't forget to find 'me' time.

Each Day, New Light

A new light to shine once again
A new vision of grief and pain
A new hope to the ignorant
A new start for the brain

A new way to open up and tell
A new excuse to part ways, to repel
A new chance to dream big
A new day to excel.

Where Am I?

In the zigzag, jumbled poetry, I am
In the folded, personalized pages, I am
I am a chirpy bird's friend
In the blue sky
In the green meadow, I am
I am with my quirky friends
In their giggles and pranks, I am
I am in the mesmerizing content of a book
In the tossed, marinated, fresh poem, I am.

A Sneak Look Outside

The archaic beauty
Why it appears so pale
Where are all the glistening grounds
And the blooming dales?

The liberty to move around freely
Where it's gone
The pick-pockets, robbers
Are ready to strike horns

The depression and anxiety today
Have replaced the placid demeanour
The trees will soon be vanished
So un-fragrant are the flowers

Let's wake people in deep slumber
Within our range
Looking out
Let's urge for a change.

The Other Side Of Today's World

The journey of life is going at its own pace
All in the crowd, so many faces to face
Vicinity to envy, cheating and malice
Making people wreck other's homes
And construct their own palaces

Unity decreasing, getting unduly individualistic
Forgetting the hard work
Faith dwindling into rituals

The rich go for boasting, the poor make a yell
Caste, religion, race on pinnacle
Mankind gone to hell

Let us be high now, let others get demotion
This race is making people insane
And making them forget emotions.

Dawn Time

The sun is rising up
Wake up, all you sleepy heads
The divine atmosphere will please you soon
Just push pillows aside
And come out of your beds
The chirping, whispering birds
Are waiting for you
To hear their cacophony
See them race along the horizon
Just take a moment to admire
The marvellous creatures of nature
Buzzing in the dawn time
Trust me
You're going to have a good day ahead.

A Day That Went Productive

A day productive feels like
Cherry on the cake like
The morning with the meals like
The pain that heals like
A frown as a smile like
Whole endeavour as one mile like
A foe as a friend like
A start as an end like
A gloomy day with light like
The animations with life like
All in all, it's a good start.

Sleep Addict, Me

My sullen stressful face
Will boost up soon
As this hectic day gets over
I feel to cash in my chips on my bed
This can surely cheer me up
Because I live in the world of fantasy
There's no strain, no pain
I like to dream, dream all day
I love to sleep, sleep again.

Trust Your Instincts

Copying moves along with people in the crowd
Keep up the ingenuity with which you're endowed
Everything is possible for the one who does believe
What difference you add to your efforts is what you receive

Ordinary are they but the one
Who is extraordinary becomes the great
Keep up the originality
Otherwise you'll plead for the lost golden dates

Everyone has the power to make people impress
In all ways
It all matters how you enhance and embellish
This art within a few days

Beautiful made by many, masterpieces by one
Keep up the originality
You'll not believe when you'll compete with the stars
And shine like the shimmering sun.

A Fresh Poem

A fresh poem is a lost friend
Lost for some time
But seems to meet in the end

Our dynamic struggle blossoms at last
Sometimes so stubborn
Sometimes so fast

I try and observe a lot
Yet it depends upon my mood
It always flourishes when alone
When left in solitude

A fresh poem always encourages me
To write many more
Always boosts up my confidence
And relaxes me from the deep core.

A Day On A Beach

On a lovely beach all set to go
A wide expanse of sand
Sea-shells scattered all over
As divine as heavenly land

The shimmering sun and gushing waves
Exciting all of us to enjoy this lovely day-out
To sit in the shade of a tree stout

The cosy breeze striking against my face
The adorable birds racing in pace
The sparkling drops of water slowly
Have made my face wet

Oh, I'll rush home the sun is about to set.

Be An Actor Not A Reactor

To wipe out the odds in life and stand erect
None of the worldly powers
Will stop you from rising
When you yourself are correct

Remember, the fools will open up
To evolve envy and enmity
But what appropriate is, to readily listen
And flush these words as of time
We run a scarcity

You'll get badly entangled in their games
If you pissed off these kindred brains
And on them you poke
But you have to turn this game
Wickedly into your favour
By smiling and understanding them as a joke

At last you'll surely win
If you never lose hope
If you scour something positive
In every negative phase of life
And if learnt from darkness to cope.

Impressions

I left a mark a few days ago
For the sodden echoes that come and go
I dream and desire to conquer the world
I'll cheer myself when suppressed and low

I want to mark with my wisdom and wit
Dreams on high, benchmark to hit
I'll make my path glow and gleam
I'll not get entangled in any tit-bits

Tremendous efforts, vision in the eyes
This is all I need in life to rise.

An Apology For My Handwriting

My school space is for me to grow
Please spare my words
They are to and fro

What's with these D's and K's
They appear so unlively
My teacher always says to me
Why can't you write elegantly?

My apologies are endless
But this time it's over
Like before
When it comes to exams
Nonetheless I score

Honestly, this pleases me a little more
At last, I promised her
I'll write better than before.

Hardships

Life is endowed with various hardships
Which keep coming like a speed breaker
Balancing over-confidence on roads to success
Handle these hurdles with patience
And always keep calm to access

The enigmatic belief will retain its bitterness
If you touch the dangling cords at times
Try not to get disheartened
In any clime

Don't care what people say
And the viewpoints they have for you
Remember, the positive vibes
Can generate within you, yourself
And can end within you

Believe these hardships as
Another chance to excel
And part ways with people
Keeping your calm repel.

Mom

She's the one to encourage us
Without being acknowledged herself
She's the one to serve us first
At the stake of starving herself

She's the one to wipe our tears
And cheer us up
Without being comforted
Without being consoled herself
She's the one to withstand us

At every phase of our life
Just for a day sit beside her
She's a mother, daughter and a wife

It's a really petty thing to think of her
As just our caretaker
She's the one and the only one
A multitasker
A perfect homemaker.

Work Consistent For Success

The bright, about to bloom bud
Will continue to flourish and grow, as long as watered
Any irregularity
Any deferring to the day after
Will cease its growth
The bright colours will begin to fade
The fright and the urge of the baby bud
If we are unable to hear
Will be ruptured, gloomy and frightened
No choice left, just to repent
We'll not be able to see
The wiggling flower
That we once dreamt of.

Embellish Up Your Future

The best way to predict the future
Is to create it
To remove the un-productivity going on
We have to shiver in the rains
Scorch in the sun
Of hard work a bit

To be the part of gaiety one day
Dedication is the only way
The clouds of defeat will themselves give up
And empty your track
Compel these clouds to rain
Fight and gain expertise in things you lack

The past is gone, the present is going
And the future is still in our hands
Stand up for winning one day
The odds of life will forever end.

My Worthy Hand

I use you to create
I use you to destroy
I use you when sad or bored
To express my joy

You're always there with me
True companion - at times
Smelly, sweaty, sticky
And so clean sometimes

With the help of yours
I'll try to beautify this world
And some ways I'll mend
I want every goal of mine set by myself
Till I have this worthy hand.

Copy, Cut and Paste

For those who think
Yes I copy, cut and paste
The words are my own
But yes I blend the taste

The ideas I reflect, I observe when alone
Yes I copy, cut and paste
The thought is my own

I scribble at last, gather ideas when bored
Yes I copy, cut and paste
But a little effort is required

Yes I copy, cut and paste
But my determination and
My dynamic struggle, need a start
Because it's nothing less than a dream
To create a piece of art.

Loneliness – A Great Phase In Life

Sometimes I like and enjoy myself sitting alone
Sometimes I think I can rule this world by sitting on a throne
Sometimes these useless and time-wasting thoughts
Surround my mind and make me lonely
But I know if I turn this loneliness into a creative day
I'll be my real self

I like to make many friends
But sometimes get worried about their intentions
That's why I like staying alone
To supervise myself, to help
Me-myself and staying away from pointless tension.

Music

Highly evocative, helps us discover
New thoughts and feelings
It soothes the heart magically
And gives it healings

Provides life to the heart
Rhythm to the soul
It's just preppy and fun
It plays a vital role

It seems to be the strumming and patting
Of the tune inside our heart
And if we hear we love it
And I for surely want to imbibe this art.

In Search of More

I enjoy the hustle
And I do want more of it
I enjoy being busy
With a pinch of friendly tit-bits

Working for myself
Is like climbing, unending mountain
After achieving I am not going to stop
I put in my best to hear sparkling fountains

After achieving even a bit
I am not going to smile and sit
I'll just do my best
Don't know, if I'll be any good at it

This hunt has given me
A lot of growth and new dreams
I am in search of more
I'll be one as a team.

Beauty Lies Within

(A small token of gratitude to my teacher Miss Nivedita Lall ma'am on Gratitude Day)

You're so adorned by God
No words needed to adorn you
You're so defined yourself
None other needs to expound you

I feel proud to have you as a preacher
I feel honoured that you're my beloved teacher

The quality liked by me
Is the simplicity you possess
To the point you speak
Not a word in excess

Your words add a lot
So does your spell-binding smile
You're as natural as possible
With élan you carry your style

As dedicated as your name
Yes, one of the rarest creature
Yes, I feel proud to be your student
I feel proud that you're my mentor.

One Grade Up-My New Classroom

It feels so liberating and exciting
To step in a new room
And beside a new window pane
To make new friends
And meet old classmates again

To take maths lightly again
To chat and to fight
To study only at the last moment
Not sleeping half the night

The pressure of final exams
Was like stepping on an undulating pebble
But now in this short break
My enthusiasm is gone to a record new level.

Look Over Your Overlooks

The pleasures neglected with them you abide
Fantasies all over are to be explored
Keep arrogance on one side

Obduracy and wickedness can
No longer make you win
Look over your mistakes
Accept them with a grin

Overlook enmity and anger
Friendship with resolve to access
Look over your overlooks
You'll no doubt achieve success.

Zero Period

Pin-drop silence, not a word do I utter
This time is for me
To know myself better

Enjoying it to the fullest
Utilising it the best
The pleasures neglected now found
That all was a long-time quest

Many fests organised, many students being a part
This is the time for me to make a good start
Syllabus to study, exams on the way
But this time is surely kept for me
With words to play.

It Makes My Day To Laugh

I'll always remember, our chatter
As I hadn't laughed in a while
Night turns in a hustle and bustle
And I even forget to smile

A hectic day is that basic dish
Where a pinch of laughter does vanish
The whole dish appears insipid
No longer worthy of relish

Laughter adds spice
To every mundane routine
As it's worth to make someone laugh
Than really to mean

Everyone's so busy, can't pass
Even an appreciable comment
Life will ever move, wait a little
Enjoy the little sweet happy moment.

A Birthday Present For A Friend

Sheer happiness, you're turning thirteen
Beware of all, that looks attractive
As you're entering the world of teens

You're important to me
Especially when having our lunch
In the interval, we share all gossips
Laugh, sit, crunch and munch

So cheerful, friendly you're
But at my sarcastic comments
A little stiff you're

Never cry, your tears are
As precious as a pearl
But when you smile and laugh
You're the most beautiful girl.

The World Is Going To Wait

A future icon, an activist, the world-reformer
When will he be born?
Each dusk, each dawn
Each time, each breath, the world is waiting

We are delayed somewhat
Let's be a little more late
For the one to change the world
The world can wait

We are lacking somewhere still
Let the youth rise
This dependence for sure
Is the reason to be late

So, let ourselves do something
While the world waits.

Our Work Lasts Forever

All the glittering gems, embellishments
Are going to say-
Man always takes his worthy aspect away

Wealth will decline one day
But the glory will last forever
We'll have to leave this world one day
But our work will stay forever

The synopsis of our achievements
Will always be there
Focus on what can be done now
For the rest least care.

Clothes Don't Make A Man

Why stick to the opinion
Made just in a while, just in an hour?
Why can't people see behind the cloud?
The long waiting for the shining star

Our dressing sense can hide the real us for some time
But our words reveal us inside out
When our words are stronger than our voice
Then no reason for sure is left to shout

We should, we must, we can
Let our words do all the magic
As clothes don't make the man.

Bonds In Life

Bonds are the threads of love and faith
Keeping us alive
They being a part of us
Protect us from all strife

They bring with them
Affection for one another
And in the ups and downs
Only these bonds really matter

Bonds just add more character to life
They make it more fun
Adding in sugar and spice.

I Agree To Be 'Me'

I give the thumbs down to negotiate
I decline to prove myself
I rule out to look behind
I refuse to puzzle my mind

I agree to grow better
I accept, I'll hit the mark
I insist to be myself
I accede to dispel the dark.

Let’s Nurture Her Together

The wretched soul still has hope
Malevolence all around, the outside world to cope
The impelling society not accepting
Her forte to success, her heart is brave
Accepting her as good for nothing
We’ll even fail to crave
She does have fire ignited in her heart
She can shatter all those, unjust ways
She is bold and daring to the core

Just nurture her
Give her a chance
You all.

Conclusion

A good conclusion
Is like drops of rain in an arid land

While an abrupt end can lead everything to the vain

That ending which gives the most relatable outcome
A topic on which we can think more and more

Scientific, logical and scholastic

A befitting conclusion is one that
Hammers home the message
And sounds didactic.

Passion Not Impulsiveness

The wishes and desires will fulfil themselves
Just what you need is some knowledge to pursue
And passion to mend
Just acquire these before it is too late
Your endeavours have no end

Some new goals appear
So overwhelming to accomplish
Some new challenges appear
So huge to challenge
Just what we need is to keep
Fluttering excitement aside
And reason, passion to balance

Research thoroughly
You'll compose your mind again
Be in low profile always
Always be sober, sincere and plain.

Frenemies

Cared a lot but now we have to move apart
Wished, you hadn't said that thing
Which deeply pinched my heart

I believe, I am as annoying as I was
I always started at first
But you gradually widened the gap between
And finally breached my trust
You tried to mislead me
And put me on a pause
You tried to back me off
And betrayed all my applause

You're my classmate still
And I am still frenemy of yours
You're good at acting though
Nevertheless I'm, for sure

Thank you so much to make me realize
You are a mistake of mine
But you proved it right
All friends don't stand through rain and sunshine

Forgive me to pissed you
And censure you here
You made me realize
That I lack somewhere.

These Supporting Shoulders- "Happy Father's Day"

That telling, thorough voice
That one, gleeful in every choice
That one, at all my wins
Is happy always, always rejoices
That power-packed smile turns
Every gloomy day to gaiety
And I am growing slowly but surely
I feel strong when dad's with me

Our tit-bits amuse me for sure
These helping hands are really sweet and pure
His fresh ideas are always energizing
And the bond we share is just mesmerizing.

List of Publication

Grateful Acknowledgements are made to the following journals in which these poems first appeared

1. What Life Teaches Us - Poetry Today - 2018 issue
2. How To Make A Good Day - Poetry Today - 2018 issue
3. Loneliness - A Great Phase In Life - Rock Pebbles - Vol. XXII No. III : September 2018 Issue
4. Words I - Contemporary Vibes -Vol. 14 - Issue No. 53 Oct-Dec 2018 Issue
5. Words II - Contemporary Vibes -Vol. 14 - Issue No. 53 Oct-Dec 2018 Issue
6. Beauty Lies Within - Bizz Buzz - Vol 20 - Issue 2018
7. Dawn Time - (IJML) Vol. 9, No. 1: January 2019 issue
8. A Day On A Beach - (IJML) Vol. 9, No. 1: January 2019 issue
9. Where Am I ? - Creation and Criticism - July-Oct 2018 Issue
10. A Sneak Look Outside - Creation and Criticism - July-Oct 2018 Issue
11. Mom - Creation and Criticism - July-Oct 2018 Issue
12. My Worthy Hand - Creation and Criticism - July-Oct 2018
13. Copy, Cut, Paste - Creation and Criticism - July-Oct 2018

DIAMOND BOOKS
NEW PUBLICATIONS
JAIL DIARY AND OTHER WRITINGS
BHAGAT SINGH
Why I am an Atheist And Other Writings
Cricket Betting And The Fake ICC World Cup 2023
Atul Kumar
MEDIA REVOLUTION 2030
VIKAS SHARMA
ROYAL HISTORY OF GURJARA DYNASTY (PART-1)
K.M. MUNSHI
ROYAL HISTORY OF GURJARA DYNASTY (PART-2)
K.M. MUNSHI
For You only
Medical Emergency
If you are the FIRST RESPONDER!
Dr. Biswaroop Roy Chowdhury
POCKET Guide
TIME MANAGEMENT IS LIFE MANAGEMENT
RINKAL SHARMA & AMIT SHARMA
75 Unsung Heroes of India
Rinkal Sharma
Forgotten Gems 75 Brave Women of India
Rinkal Sharma
Eating Out at Home
Mona Asoka Verma
DAL FOODS OF INDIA
MONA ASOKA VERMA
FASTING FOODS OF INDIA
MONA ASOKA VERMA
The Ultimate DAL Cook Book
Mona Asoka Verma
DIAMOND BOOKS
X-30, Okhla Industrial Area, Phase-II New Delhi-110020
Ph: 011-40712200 email : wecare@diamondbooks.in www.diamondbooks.in